MW00604578

KANSAS
Then&Now

Monroe Dodd

New photography by
Jean Dodd and Monroe Dodd

KANSAS CITY STAR BOOKS
KANSAS CITY, MISSOURI

Published by Kansas City Star Books
1729 Grand Boulevard
Kansas City, MO 64108

First edition
ISBN: 9781611690439
Library of Congress Control Number: 2012904309

Book designer: Jean D. Dodd

Dust jacket illustrations: Front cover, Paola, north side of square, early 1860s
and the same scene today. Back cover, clockwise from top, Coronado Heights;
Mullinville Round Barn; Monument Rocks; Fox Theater, Salina; Main Street,
Ottawa.

Introductory photographs: i, Grand opening of Union Pacific Depot,
Marysville, 1928; ii, Kansas Pacific locomotive, Wallace, 1873; iii, brick
found in authors' travels; iv-v, McPherson, early 1930s; iv, Topeka, 1863.

Printed in the United States of America
by Walsworth Publishing Co. Inc., Marceline, Mo.

Order online at www.TheKansasCityStore.com or call StarInfo at (816) 234-
4636 and say "operator."

CONTENTS

PREFACE

Look at any historical picture — say, one from the 1870s, filled with buggies and horses and people in frontier garb. Then, find that place today and look around. You'll see differences, but people in both scenes are walking the same ground, literally and figuratively. They wear different clothes and travel in different ways, yet their inner lives are much alike. They feel love and hate, do good deeds and bad ones, have envy and pride. Use a little imagination, and in that spot you can visit the past, do a bit of time-traveling.

Kansas Then & Now can help with the journey. It covers the state from east to west and in between, showing what Kansas looked like through the century and a half since statehood and what it looks like today.

For this book, we found scenes from Kansas' past — from the 1850s and territorial days to the late 20th century. We stood as close as possible to the places where the original photographers stood, and then took pictures. In a few of those places, momentous events occurred and famous people strode the earth. But more often we found everyday places featuring everyday people who did a most extraordinary thing: They created communities out of prairie and plain.

Kansas is a big place. Whether a Kansan lives in the heart of the state, or on the edges, or in the corners, the view of the rest of it too often is shaped by what's outside the car window. That view, at 75 mph on the way somewhere else, reveals little. In most communities, the motorist sees only the outliers— gasoline stations, convenience stores, fast-food restaurants and motels. From Interstate 35, a driver can't see Ottawa's Main Street, or the courthouse square in El Dorado. From Interstate 70, there's no view of the parade ground at old Fort Hays or downtown Abilene.

Once we began this project, that narrow view changed. Off the main highway, rattling down a brick Main Street, circling a courthouse square, poking around an old rail yard, we learned much more. Usually we met a local person who knew another local person who was interested in local history. Right away, whether it was Goodland or Garden City, Paola or Pittsburg, we were overwhelmed with help and suggestions — not to mention historic photographs.

The "Then" images, naturally, came first. We matched every old scene as nearly as possible with a "Now." Sometimes, we had little idea where the old scenes were photographed. Evocative scenes of cowboys or harvests or chuck wagons in the 1890s came labeled only with the name of a county or a landowner, and we had to eliminate them. Other scenes were impossible to replicate because something more recent stood in the way — a new building or a wall or a tree.

Nevertheless, we found abundant possibilities and went to the sites to capture the "Now." We began in late 2011 and finished in early 2012. It did not take long for us to realize the problem would be not acquiring enough usable images, but narrowing them down to fit the reasonable constraints of a book.

This book is organized in chronological order, by the date of the historical photographs. Some photos bore marks identifying them down to the day they were taken. Many were not even identified by year. At times we had to estimate based on the best evidence — styles of dress and of conveyances, store names in city directories or old maps.

This is the fourth volume published by Kansas City Star Books in which scenes of yesterday are compared to the same scenes today. The first three books covered the Kansas City area, and many Kansas Citians were familiar with those views. Few Kansans, we suspect, and even fewer non-Kansans are familiar with all these.

For us, finding the photos, determining where they were taken and photographing them as they are today usually led to an interesting detective mystery, a search for clues, and eventually a date with some small parcel of the past.

Welcome, then, to Kansas of the past and the present. The trip requires you to pack only one item: Your imagination.

Monroe Dodd

1856-1869

Kansas' earliest settlers promptly built communities. They drew boundaries and lot lines, bought and sold properties and built homes and stores. Leavenworth, Atchison, Quindaro and other towns sprang up just across the border from Missouri. Farther west, along the Kansas River, emigrants laid out streets and put up buildings in Topeka and Lawrence. By March 1856, barely two years after Kansas was declared a territory, the Massachusetts Street business district of Lawrence was taking form, left. The view was south from today's Sixth Street. The three-story Free State Hotel, still weeks away from its opening, stood on the right or west side of Massachusetts. The photographer positioned his equipment inside an earthen embankment intended to help defend the anti-slavery community from attack. Nevertheless, attacks came.

The city symbol is a phoenix rising from the ashes. Twice Lawrence had to come back from destruction – the first time only months after the early photograph was made. On May 21,1856, pro-slavery partisans led by the Douglas County sheriff, Samuel Jones, destroyed the Free State Hotel by fire and cannon blast. They burned at least one house, broke up printing presses of two newspapers and perpetrated various other looting and vandalism. Seven years afterward came the far bloodier and costlier attack by the guerrilla band of William C. Quantrill. Each time, the city's economy recovered nicely. The memories, however, never died. Above: Today's Massachusetts Street, south from Sixth.

ATCHISON
• 1859

A national political candidate had good reason to visit distant Kansas Territory late in 1859, almost a year before the presidential election. Among other things, he could trot out his ideas far from the big eastern newspapers and their reporters. If western audiences didn't like a speech, few would know it. So Abraham Lincoln, an Illinois lawyer who had made a name in debate, accepted an invitation from friends in the territory, traveled through Missouri by train and on November 30 crossed the river into Kansas. He traveled by carriage in bitter cold from town to town along the western side of the river – from Elwood to Troy to Doniphan and then, on Friday, December 2, to Atchison. Here, he spoke in this rather modest Methodist church building, only eight months old, which stood on a block bounded by Fifth, Sixth, Parallel and Laramie streets. At the time, the church was the largest hall available in the town. Officials of the congregation, it is said, acceded only grudgingly to the use of the building for Lincoln's speech. The speech, however, went well; after talking for an hour and a half, Lincoln indicated he would wind things up, but the crowd urged him on — and on he went, for at least another half-hour.

ATCHISON
• 2012

Lincoln departed Atchison the next morning, December 3, 1859. He went to Leavenworth, spoke there and then returned east across the Missouri River. The ideas he tried out in Kansas, as it happened, went over well in the rest of the country and in November 1860 he was elected president. Lincoln never traveled farther west than he did that cold December night in Atchison. As for the building where he spoke, the Methodist congregation departed for larger quarters in the early 1870s. The building was taken down and homes went up on the block, which today sits across the street from the Atchison County Courthouse.

Kansas was still a territory in 1860 when this scene was captured. The view is southwest past the hardware store at Fourth and Commercial streets, Atchison's business hub. The city was five years old at the time, and in its early years its economy benefitted from steamboat traffic on the Missouri River and from overland trade — routes extended to the West Coast. The proximity of Atchison to Missouri meant the city contained a substantial number of pro-slavery residents. In fact, it took its name from a pro-slavery Missouri senator, David Rice Atchison.

The Civil War ended the question of slavery, and the building of the first railroad bridge across the Missouri River at Kansas City in 1869 ended the matter of which city would dominate the region. Nevertheless, Atchison's active pursuit of railroads and manufacturing kept it a growing and lively place through the 19th century.

This army post was the first place organized and occupied by European-Americans in what would become Kansas. Fort Leavenworth was established in 1827 to watch over Indian tribes that were being moved to the territory west of Missouri and also to escort traders on the commercial road to Santa Fe. Thirty-five years later, in 1862, this photograph was taken. Lined up at left-shoulder arms on the main parade ground was Company F of the year-old Eighth Kansas Volunteer Infantry, recruited to protect the new state of Kansas and its border with Missouri during the Civil War. The company's main task was to chase Missouri guerrilla raiders. Company F eventually would join other companies of the Eighth Kansas where the war was happening — in the South.

Today, the main parade ground where Company F lined up for its picture is filled with trees and bordered by officers' residences. The two houses in the center and left background are still standing. They are called the Syracuse houses after the home town of the architect who was imported to build them. Fort Leavenworth continues as an active military post, home to the Combined Arms Center and the Command and General Staff College.

As they did in Lawrence, New Englanders and their anti-slavery sentiments dominated this settlement in its early years. Like several other towns in the 1850s, Topeka served as a site for a constitutional convention in the territory. When statehood arrived in 1861, Topeka became the capital and waited out the Civil War, then began growing. Meanwhile, buildings went up along and near its main street, Kansas Avenue. These businesses served a pioneer clientele with feed and gear for horses, seed for farmers and meat for townspeople. As in other early Kansas towns, wood and stone composed the basic building materials.

After the Civil War, wood buildings were demolished and stone structures took their places along Kansas Avenue. The streetscape changed more than once.

Today, the multiple buildings have been replaced by a single structure housing offices of a bank.

Along Massachusetts Street, lots filled in rapidly in the years just before and after statehood. Visible in this view to the north from today's Eighth Street are signs for businesses selling boots and shoes, stoves, hardware and baked goods. People wearing heavy coats have gathered with their mounts on the west side of the street. Neatness and order were not observed strictly on Massachusetts, which is strewn with casks, boxes and a trunk.

Business streets in most Kansas towns evolved based on the success or failure of merchants; Massachusetts Street underwent a drastic change in 1863 because of war. That August guerrillas under the command of William Quantrill raided the town from Missouri, killing nearly 150 men and boys, destroying much of this business district and burning hundreds of homes. The next year, however, brought the railroad and with the end of war in 1865 prosperity returned — as did the commercial district of Lawrence. Today, Massachusetts Street continues to thrive.

Mules and covered wagons were a common site in Kansas towns in the 1860s, and on this day the northern part of Paola's city square teemed with freighters. The same photographer who captured this scene from the second floor of a store at the northeast corner of the square also took a portrait of Union General James G. Blunt and his band in 1864, standing next to the two-story, three-pillared building in the middle of the block. The best evidence is that these bandsmen replaced those who had been slaughtered by Quantrill's guerrillas at Baxter Springs the year before.

PAOLA • 2012

Brick buildings line Peoria Street on the north side of Paola's square today. The structure in the center of the block and behind Blunt's band members in the 1860s photographs still stands — it's the one with the green awning — but its pillars, porch and balcony have been replaced by a brick façade. Not visible from this angle are the original stone walls of the structure.

Two horsemen steadied their mounts for a Civil War portrait on the parade ground at Fort Scott in Bourbon County. The fort was established in 1842, one of a line of installations along the American frontier from Louisiana to Minnesota. Its job was to keep the peace in an area where there was no local government or law. In 1855, once Kansas Territory was established, the fort was abandoned and its buildings sold, forming the center of a new town, also called Fort Scott. When the Civil War began, the Union Army took back control of its old buildings and built new ones for an expanded fort. Some refugees from the vicious clashes along the Kansas-Missouri border joined the Union Army here.

The Army left for good in 1873, and the city of Fort Scott grew in and around the old fort structures. Some military buildings were demolished, others were altered and a few survived. In the middle 20th century, a group of residents campaigned to have the post restored. With federal backing the fort was reopened in 1978 as a national historic site and today it is operated by the National Park Service.

This was Kansas' first city and its most prosperous from the opening of Kansas Territory in 1854 through much of the 1860s, drawing merchants and residents to its bustling downtown. A stack of bricks sat in Delaware Street, ready for new construction. Furniture stores, drugstores, a cobbler's shop, a carriage maker, confectioners and cigar stores lined the block in this view from Fifth Street east toward the Missouri River. The photographer was Alexander Gardner, who was hired by the Union Pacific Railroad, Eastern Division, to document the region along the route. A side trip brought him to Leavenworth. The railroad later was renamed the Kansas Pacific.

The city's hopes to hold the front rank in the region were dashed in the late 1860s when railroads chose to begin a cross-Kansas line at Wyandotte (today part of Kansas City) and then chose Kansas City, Missouri, as the spot for the first bridge across the Missouri River. Leavenworth's population and business growth continued for a while and then cooled as some businesses and residents left for the larger city downriver. Few of the 1860s buildings remain in their entirety, but Delaware Street retains a historic appearance because of structures built in the 1880s and in the early 20th century.

Alexander Gardner, the railroad photographer, photographed Fifth Street stretching down to Three Mile Creek and up the hill beyond. The First Methodist Church at left dominated the immediate scene; in the distance on the left side of the street stood the Catholic cathedral, which was under construction and still lacking two landmark spires. The large building on the skyline to the right was the public school.

Although business and residential activity in Leavenworth have shifted over the years, the city has got along well thanks in part to a large federal presence at the Army fort, penitentiary and veterans' hospital, along with Hallmark cards and other private employers. Along Fifth Street, more modest buildings have replaced the Methodist church, the cathedral and the school of the 1860s.

Six years after statehood and two years after the end of the Civil War, work was under way on a new Capitol in Topeka. The site was donated by local boosters headed by Cyrus K. Holliday. Alexander Gardner photographed the progress on today's East Wing, the first part built. The cornerstone had been laid less than a year before. State workers began occupying the building in 1869, but it took more than three decades for the building to be finished

TOPEKA
• 2012

Behind a chain link fence, construction work continued as part of a 21st-century renovation of the structure — from the dome to new offices underground. The work began in the early 2000s.

When the Union Pacific, Eastern Division, entered Manhattan from the east, it had to bridge the Blue River in the foreground. At that point, the Blue was only a few yards from its mouth at the Kansas River. Alexander Gardner stationed his camera on the bridge above the stream and pointed it nearly due west down Manhattan's Poyntz Avenue. As with most Kansas towns of the period, a few substantial stone buildings stood among hastily assembled wood-frame structures, one of which bore a sign, "Cheap Cash Store."

Because of heavy flooding in the first two decades of the 20th century, the Blue River changed its course. Today, it enters the Kansas River about a mile and a half downstream to the east, and the old bed of the Blue has been filled with earth. Heavily traveled streets, Tuttle Creek and Fort Riley boulevards and East Poyntz Avenue, meet there, and the area is home to motels, restaurants and car dealers.

As the Union Pacific, Eastern Division, made its way west across Kansas employees came upon these geological oddities less than a mile south of the track. The Dakota sandstone concretions resulted from centuries of weathering. They began as beach sands and sediments 66 to 144 million years before, when the area was sea and coastline. This rock and another to the north resembled mushrooms. On this day, photographer Gardner and his party dropped by to take pictures and pose.

In the 1960s, the five acres on which this and other curious rock formations appear was donated to the Kansas Department of Wildlife and Parks by the Ellsworth County Historical Society. The area is called Mushroom Rock State Park. It is about six miles east of Kanopolis.

After the Civil War, as railroads, land speculators, farmers and ranchers and others with a bit of wanderlust began to look west, the federal government established military outposts across Kansas. The forts served as the advance guard of the American settlers, meant to protect them from Indian attack. Fort Hays guarded the Smoky Hill Trail, which ran from Atchison to Denver and cut right through prime hunting lands of Cheyenne, Arapahoe, Sioux, Pawnee, Kiowa and Comanches. Established in October 1865 as Fort Fletcher, by the next year the post had moved a short distance and its name had been changed to Fort Hays. In this scene, the Fifth Infantry band stood on the parade ground in front of officers' row.

Like most of the forts built to protect settlers — Larned, Harker, Wallace, Dodge and others — the heyday of Fort Hays lasted only from the late 1860s to the early 1870s. Unlike most of those others, Fort Hays remained open until the late 1880s, although in later years the garrison spent its time maintaining the buildings. In the 20th century, the land was turned over to the state for an agricultural research center. The predecessor of Fort Hays State University began classes in the old fort hospital in 1902 and then moved north to the site of the present campus. Some of the officers' quarters were sold and moved into nearby Hays; two of them were moved back when a state historic park was created on the property. Restored, these stand on original sites.

1870-1899

WICHITA • 1870 and 2012

When it was platted, left, Wichita had only a few buildings, a few wagons, a few horses and men and mostly flat countryside in the plain of the Arkansas River. The first wood-frame buildings were under construction in 1870 on the west side of Main Street, north of Douglas Avenue.

Above: After the railroad reached here, Wichita became a new cow capital. Like other towns temporarily at the head of the rails, it boomed and then slowed as farmers fenced the land, the railroads kept building and the cattle herds were redirected farther west. With the growth of wheat farming and eastern investments, Wichita was energized again in the late 1800s, emerging as a milling and grain-trading center.

37

Buffalo hunting accomplished several goals for early settlers of Barton County. The animals provided food and also hides that could be tanned and sold. The vast herds also trampled crops, so reducing their number may have been viewed as a way to make farming easier. These hunters lined up in front of the county's grand new courthouse, built in 1873. The city took its name from the big bend of the Arkansas River nearby.

The city went through a cow-capital phase in the 1870s, with all the rowdiness and thuggery that era entailed, and then the Kansas Legislature restricted the cattle drives to points farther west. Great Bend became a regional shopping and trading hub, and in the 1930s and 1940s a center of oil production. The original courthouse was replaced by this four-story beaux-arts structure built in 1917 and 1918.

Still not big enough to be called a city, Wichita in its first half-decade retained an Old West, small-town appearance. Wood-frame buildings with false fronts, intermittent wood sidewalks and dirt streets marked the first block of North Main .

This block now features a big-city countenance. An imposing bank building sits on the west side of North Main where once Black & Nixon and others sold groceries and hardware.

BROOKVILLE • 1873

ON THE KANSAS PACIFIC RAILWAY.
No. 30. Kansas Pacific Railway Roundhouse and Company's
Buildings at Brookville, Kansas.
PHOTO. BY R. BENECKE, ST. LOUIS, MO.

Not only the rails themselves but also the advent of railroad shops angered native Americans, to whom the buildings symbolized encroachment on hunting lands. After this roundhouse was built in central Kansas in 1867 and the town of Brookville developed, Indians attacked, driving people inside the roundhouse and threatening to set it ablaze. As the story goes, a railroad crew fired up a steam locomotive and smashed it through the doors, scattering the attackers and heading to Salina for aid.

A single Union Pacific track passes by Brookville today, outside this photo to the left. It parallels Kansas 140, which is to the right. This grassy area remains where the roundhouse, turntable and shops once stood. The railroad moved its operation to Junction City in the late 1880s. West of this spot, an early hotel survived for more than a century as a family-owned fried-chicken restaurant, housed in an Old-West-style front and called simply the Brookville Hotel. In the last decade the family moved the operation to Abilene.

The University of Kansas opened in September 1866, in a small building on the north end of Mount Oread. Enrollment was 55 men and women. By 1872, the university dedicated a bigger structure, at first called simply the New Building.

Five years later, it had become known as University Hall and in 1897 it was named Fraser Hall after a former chancellor

To the dismay of preservationists, old Fraser Hall was demolished in 1965 and a new, larger Fraser built in its place. The university's enrollment has climbed past 25,000.

This was the Wild West, not a play-acted gunfight but the actual bodies of two soldiers, Privates Peter Walsh (alternately spelled "Welsh") and George Summer (alternately "Sumner"), who were shot to death outside Cy Goddard's saloon and dance hall on September 6, 1873. Their assailant was a fellow trooper in the Sixth Cavalry, David Roberts. A curious child watched over the scene.

HAYS • 2011

Cy Goddard's saloon closed in 1876 and the buildings that replaced it along 10th Street have themselves been supplanted by a massive brick structure. Bronze plaques mark historic sites in downtown Hays. Many, like the one at this spot, describe saloons, brothels and gambling houses of former days.

WALLACE • 1873

This western Kansas town was established next to the military reservation of Fort Wallace, which was established right after the Civil War to protect travelers on the Smoky Hill Trail. First, those travelers rode the coaches of the Butterfield Overland Dispatch but in 1867 the railroad arrived. Six years later, this hotel, along with a depot and shops, had been built. This picture was made by a photographer hired by the Kansas Pacific railroad.

The railroad moved its operations west in 1890 and business in the town of Wallace slackened. Grain elevators now tower over the area where the depot and hotel once stood. The town survived, and on its east side a historical museum welcomes visitors along U.S. 40.

This town epitomized the Old West in legend, preserved in pulp fiction, movies, television and word of mouth. Much of the legend was based in fact. First came Fort Dodge in 1865 and, five miles away and seven years later, the town itself. Buffalo hunters and freighters on the Santa Fe Trail traded at the small community, which in August 1872 was organized and named after the fort. Within a month, the railroad arrived. Cowboys, trainmen and buffalo hunters made Dodge a wild and woolly place. At Frederick Zimmerman's hardware store, the sale and servicing of firearms stood first among the offerings.

Front Street still sells gear and provides entertainment, but for years it has catered to Old West tourists instead of cowboys and buffalo hunters.

The people posing for the photographer look peaceful enough, but the clientele served by these establishments could become very rowdy, indeed. Policing was required and some of the Old West's most famous lawmen spent time in Dodge City, among them Bat Masterson and Wyatt Earp.

Front Street's original wood buildings were removed after the city began to settle down in the 1880s. In succeeding years, local boosters realized the tourist potential and built a recreation of original Front Street a few blocks west.

This was the first Kansas cattle town to receive herds of longhorns and ship them east, thanks to Joseph G. McCoy. In 1867 McCoy established a stockyards in this tiny community, which had just become the end of the Union Pacific, Eastern Division, later the Kansas Pacific. From here livestock was shipped to stockyards in Kansas City. That made Abilene a regular destination for rough-and-tough Texas cowboys, who drank and caroused to their hearts' content for a couple of years as the town tried out various lawmen — among them Wild Bill Hickok. By the early 1870s, the rowdy situation took care of itself. Rail heads moved south and west, the countryside around Abilene was settled and farms fenced. The drovers took their business elsewhere and Abilene concentrated on agricultural pursuits.

In the 1940s, long after its claim to Wild West fame ended, Abilene grabbed attention again as the hometown of the man who led Allied forces to victory in Europe in World War II and then became president, Dwight D. Eisenhower. His Museum and Library here have long been a draw for tourists and historians.

This was the livestock emporium that lay at the other end of the cattle trade from Abilene and other towns. The Kansas City livestock exchange stood in the midst of the 55-acre Kansas City stockyards, all of which lay in Kansas, squeezed between the Kansas River and the Missouri state line. This building succeeded a wood-frame structure that housed the trading activity when Joseph McCoy inspired the beginning of the cross-state commerce.

The exchange was enlarged several times in Kansas. In 1895 it expanded across the line into Missouri after the Kansas Legislature began investigating the stockyards' practices. In 1911, the Livestock Exchange moved wholly into Missouri. By the 1990s, the last cattle had departed and the once-extensive livestock pens were dismantled. Of the 1876 exchange, nothing remains.

FORT LARNED • 1879 and 2012

Like other frontier forts built after the Civil War, Larned was a base for the U.S. Army to protect travelers on the Santa Fe Trail from Indians who distrusted American settlers' push into their hunting ground. From the fort, cavalry troopers patrolled the trail 70 miles in either direction. Construction of its stone buildings began in 1865. By the time this photograph was made, the coming of the railroad had reduced the use of the Santa Fe Trail, and only a small guard force protected the fort.

The National Park Service proudly calls Fort Larned the best-preserved frontier fort in the country. It now operates as a National Historic Site, established in 1964.

The landmark Chase County Courthouse was built in 1873. Its eastern-trained architect, John G. Haskell of Lawrence, chose a Second Empire style for the limestone building, which sits atop a hill at the end of Cottonwood Falls' primary business street, Broadway. Haskell also prepared the original designs for the state Capitol in Topeka. The name of this Flint Hills town came from a waterfall in the Cottonwood River near the other end of Broadway.

The building is the oldest operating courthouse in Kansas, and is a tourist draw.

Dodge City was becoming a bit citified by the early 1880s, the evidence of which was a brick building on once-wild Front Street. Men in suits replaced drovers hanging around the sidewalk and even Fred Zimmerman's hardware store had reduced its advertising of firearms; the wooden rifle that once stood on a post in front had been removed to the top of the façade. Indeed, the district put up a sign "strictly" prohibiting carrying of firearms. Prickly Ash Bitters was a patent medicine manufactured in St. Louis and billed as a purgative.

For decades, Kansas was a "dry" state and stories were told about drugstore operators who sold alcoholic concoctions for medicinal purposes. Was Prickly Ash Bitters such an elixir?

Despite Kansas' reputation as a tornado hotbed, most residents rarely see a twister. Rarer yet — until the advent of inexpensive, lightweight cameras — were photographs of tornadoes. That makes this image remarkable as well as dramatic. Taken with a large and heavy box camera in an era before fast shutter speeds, this was the first known photographic image of a tornado. A. A. Adams had time to set up his equipment in a street late the afternoon of April 26 because the tornado stayed on the ground outside Garnett about a half-hour. The town is in southeast Kansas.

GARNETT • 2012

The Presbyterian church on the right side of the 1884 photograph, its steeple altered over the years, is now the home of a community theater group.

Construction of Kansas' statehouse went on for decades; the state built it on a pay-as-you-go basis. Government operated out of today's east wing, at left, until 1881, when the west wing was finished. A covered board walkway connected the two structures for a while. In 1884, the center portion began to take shape and by the time this photograph was made the dome was rising above it all. Not until 1903 was the work finished and the final bill paid.

Most capitols demand art, and in Kansas the demands often conflicted, depending on political winds. The first murals painted inside shocked some with female nudity and they were erased. In the 1930s objections were raised to John Steuart Curry's murals for various reasons, and for decades a dispute dragged on over what should sit atop the dome. Finally, in 2002 a sculpture of a Kansa warrior was mounted there.

Pawnee County in southwest Kansas was organized in 1872, named for the Indian nation that once used the area as a hunting ground. The city of Larned was incorporated soon afterward and named the seat. This courthouse was built in the 1880s. By 1887, a brick jail had replaced the house next door.

The courthouse itself was replaced by the current courthouse at Seventh and Broadway soon after World War I.

As settlement moved west across Kansas in the late 1800s, new counties were formed and one question inevitably came to the forefront; Where will the county seat be? The courthouse and county offices would follow the choice of a seat, meaning money and influence for the winner. One of many "county seat wars" was fought out right here, in the middle of Seward County in southwest Kansas. Springfield won in a back-and-forth tussle with Fargo Springs, and the brand-new, two story Windsor Hotel helped symbolize the civic victory.

The Rock Island railroad saw things differently. It sent tracks not through Springfield but through Liberal, 16 miles south near the Oklahoma border. In 1892 the county seat moved to Liberal and so did people and businesses.

Springfield withered. Today, nothing remains of the one-time county seat, although a historical marker describes its fate. Where the hotel and town sat is now a highway rest area.

This store's location in far western Kansas gave it one big advantage. Sitting hundreds of miles from Denver or Kansas City, it could charge higher prices for goods. Peter Robidoux did just that, and made an excellent living, as did another merchant in this small town, Thomas Madigan. Both merchants kept expanding — until the railroad pulled its shops out of Wallace. As business declined, Peter Robidoux vowed he would close the day he made no sales. That day came in 1893, and he shut the doors of his emporium for good.

Investments in land and other opportunities meant neither Robidoux nor Madigan nor their families went hungry. Today, Robidoux's fancy home a few blocks away, built in 1909, is a landmark in Wallace. His store, which sat vacant for years, has been demolished.

This Graham County town was surveyed in 1879, incorporated in 1882 and named not for its location but for its founder, W. R. Hill. A competing town three miles to the southwest, Millbrook, was the original county seat but in 1887, it was wiped out by high winds. The next year, Hill City sought and won the seat, bringing new businesses to its new courthouse square. E. E. Chipman moved his drugstore from Millbrook to Hill City to follow the trade. Next door, the Elm House advertised itself with a picture of a man shouldering a log — an elm log?

Few century-old wood-frame structures remain around courthouse squares in Kansas towns, and Hill City is no exception.

A small group of southwest Kansas land speculators and promoters laid out a townsite along the Atchison, Topeka and Santa Fe tracks in the late 1870s and persuaded the rail executives to place a depot there. In the early 1880s a land office opened and hordes of developers and homesteaders descended upon the new town. Garden City was off and running. The late 1880s brought fine improvements like these along the 400 block of Main Street: the Grand Central Hotel, at left; the Opera House, the three-story building in the middle of the block, and the Windsor Hotel, right.

Once the land boom ended, the city turned to quieter but more stable pursuits – sugar-beet processing, other agriculture and cattle-feeding. The Windsor Hotel building survives, as do the first and second floors of the Grand Central Hotel.

The U.S. Army opened Fort Riley in 1853 and by the late 1860s it was one of nine forts used to defend settlers and railroad workers. In the late 19th century, athletic contests helped fill the time for cavalrymen and other soldiers stationed at the central Kansas post. Sometimes the troopers played baseball and other times raced each other. This exercise appears to have tested both strength and speed; participants rolled wagon wheels across a yard amid the cavalry barracks.

Now, only Riley and Leavenworth remain of the nine frontier forts in Kansas. Part of the barracks grounds of the 1890s has been paved for a parking lot. The buildings that once housed barracks still stand, but their sheltered balconies have been removed from this side. The fort was a training ground for thousands of doughboys in World War I and continues as an active military post.

The Dalton gang meant to knock over this bank and one across the street — a double bank robbery, in the same town on the same day, October 5, 1892. The townspeople of Coffeyville sniffed out the plot, however, and were ready for them. Grat Dalton, Jack Moore and Williams Powers entered this building, the Condon Bank. Bob and Emmett Dalton walked into the First National Bank across the street. Within minutes, townspeople began firing into the banks. Trying to escape, four members of the gang died; only Emmett survived. Four residents also died.

This city has preserved the ornate Condon Bank building, marking its most legendary hour. Within a decade after the failed Dalton raid, Coffeyville became the hub of a rich petroleum-producing area stretching from southern Kansas into nearby Oklahoma.

Their trophies lining the street and roofs, these rabbit hunters posed on a winter day in downtown Garden City. Mass hunts were a popular pastime around the turn of the century and organizers counted 416 carcasses as a result of this one.

At the corner of Main and Chestnut streets today, an awards and gift company and a barbershop operate where harness shop and lunchroom once stood.

It was branding time at these small stockyards beside the Rock Island railroad in southwest Kansas' Clark County.

Cattle remain an important industry in this part of Kansas, but the yards and slaughter houses have concentrated in Garden City and Dodge City. As symbolized by the grain elevators, wheat farming is a mainstay of the local economy.

Settled in the 1860s, this town made a living as a center for farming, particularly for dairy products. Washington County, in north central Kansas next to the Nebraska border, was one of the first 33 counties devised by the territorial legislature, but was not settled until 1860. The county, of which this is the seat, grew rapidly until the 1890s, when its population peaked at almost 23,000.

Barely a quarter of the 1890 population lives in Washington County today, but downtown Washington retains many of the structures from its boom years.

A group of Taos Indians, trying to escape harsh rule by Spanish colonial authorities in today's New Mexico, traveled to this spot in 1664, settled with Apaches and stayed for several years. In that time, they built a small pueblo reminiscent of the one they left behind. It has become known as El Cuartelejo.

The Apaches continued living here until the 1720s when, after incursions by other tribes, it was abandoned. The people in this picture possibly are local Scott County farmers who told paleontologists about the site, which is on the High Plains in western Kansas.

The ruins of the seven-room pueblo — northernmost known example of the pueblo architecture — were excavated in 1898 and in 1971 they were restored.

They lie within Lake Scott State Park. When the pueblo walls were built in the 1600s, they were made of local stone covered with adobe.

RICHLAND · 1899

Founded in 1854 along the Wakarusa River in southeast Shawnee County, this town was the birthplace of Georgia Neese, whose father was a banker in Richland. As Georgia Neese Clark, she was named the first female treasurer of the United States by President Harry S. Truman, meaning her name appeared on U.S. currency produced through most of his second term. She later married Andrew Gray and became known as Georgia Neese Clark Gray.

A ghost town in every respect, drivers on this road might have no clue that Richland existed. In the 1970s, as the Corps of Engineers made plans for Clinton Lake, Richland was determined to lie in the floodplain and it was abandoned.

Beneath the embankment on which today's S.E. 99th Street runs is the route of the old main street. Only some broken concrete remains of the town. The view is to the west.

1900-1909

A scarcity of lumber on the High Plains of western Kansas meant the first settlers had to use local materials, and in the late 1800s that material was often sod. The sod schoolhouse at left, District 22 of Thomas County, was constructed in 1886 about nine miles south of Colby. The sod walls went up first and then, using lumber imported from Oakley, the roof framing was put in place. The roof itself consisted of more sod.

Above: Rain, snow and wind were hard on sod structures, and so were farmers who want to plant fencerow to fencerow. District 22's building was replaced by a wooden one in the early 20th century and that building has since been replaced by plowed ground. A metal disc reading "Soddy School – Dist. 22" attached to a nearby utility pole is the only evidence that a school existed here.

ATCHISON • about 1900

Atchison prospered in its first decades as a transportation depot for overland travel and shipping. Steamboats unloaded at its riverfront and freight companies like the Butterfield Overland Dispatch took goods the rest of the way across the continent. Then came the railroads, among them the Atchison, Topeka and Santa Fe. By the time this photograph was made, a viaduct carried Sixth Street across multiple tracks; on the right stood the brick Missouri Pacific freight depot.

In the 20th century the city built its economy on manufacturing and milling, but transportation remained important. The city's most famous product, aviatrix Amelia Earhart, was the daughter of a railroad lawyer.

Main Street looking North   Ottawa, Kansas.

A horseless carriage appeared on Main Street with a horsedrawn buggy right behind, evidence of the coming transition in American transportation. At this date, automobiles remained expensive and few in number on the streets of Ottawa — or anywhere else. The passengers' fashionable clothing suggested that this car was owned by people of means.

In the early 1920s, automobile prices dropped to within the reach of many Americans and cars took over the streets. Now a horse is a rare sight on Main Street.

FORT SCOTT
• early 1900s and 2012

This building on the corner of Main and Wall streets began in 1874 as the Davidson Opera House and continued as a theater until the middle 1910s. It also contained various banks. Here, it's the home of First National Bank. Its president, Grant Hornaday, had his name emblazoned at the cornice.

A sign on the side of the refaced building advertises retail and office space and a tanning salon.

HILL CITY • about 1900 and 2012

The move of the county seat in 1888 and the arrival of the railroad called for Hill City to build hotels, such as the Pomeroy, which could house 75 guests. Its dining room seated 50. The hotel was built by and named for J. P. Pomeroy, a land developer who owned tens of thousands of acres in Graham County and elsewhere in northwest Kansas. Pomeroy, who had helped persuaded the railroad to build to Hill City, also gave the city a park and the county money for the courthouse.

Some of the buildings around the courthouse square are vacant but the Pomeroy's first floor still contains a second-hand store.

A railroad section crew mounted locomotive 1429 for a group portrait. The locomotive sat on the turntable at the Santa Fe repair yards roundhouse, just northwest of the Santa Fe depot.

A grassy plot and a few small trees are all that's visible where the rail yard used to be. The railroad gave the nearby depot to the Franklin County Historical Society in 1962 and the next year it was opened as a museum.

Styled in Romanesque Revival, this three-story opera house was meant to call attention to itself when it was built in 1888. The auditorium had two balconies and could seat 900 people.

Local preservationists saved the building from destruction in the middle 1980s. Over the years it was restored bit by bit. It reopened in 2010 and today the Opera House regularly offers stage acts and music — comedies, pop music tributes, concerts, free films. In its variety of entertainments the bill resembles the kinds of things opera houses offered a century ago, only updated.

As the 20th century rolled around, Larned, like its sister cities in Kansas, served farmers and ranchers with grain dealers, harness shops, banks, meat markets, blacksmiths, jewelers, druggists and sundry other businesses — not the least of which were hardware and home appliance dealers.

Appliances and other tools for living have changed over a century, but in Larned the Doerrs name on the hardware outlet has not.

Day or night, if you headed north on Commercial, Emporia's main north-south street, you got a reminder: Emporia is The Place. Town-boosting was all the rage in those days. The automobile era had not dawned, so curbside parking was crowded with carriages on a day warm enough for the boy at right center to walk barefoot, however tentatively, across the brick pavement of Commercial Street.

The modest courthouse of the early 1900s has been replaced by the Lyon County government complex, right, that covers the entire stretch along Commercial Street from Fourth to Fifth Avenues. On the left, or west side of the block, at least one building remains from a century ago, the tallest with fairly elaborate cornice.

Opened in 1882 and dedicated to the rather eclectic uses of opera house, city offices and fire station, this grand structure was seriously damaged by fire in 1898. In this view, the building had been renovated and reopened; the opera house was to the rear, faced in limestone and on this date showing a production called "Dan Cupid." The front portion, faced in brick, contained city departments, among them the firefighting force. A hook-and-ladder vehicle posed out front for this portrait.

City offices moved out of the building in 1937 and part of it operated as a movie theater. In that time, the brick was painted white. The movie theater closed in 1982 but with the turn of the 21st century came a major restoration. Now called the C.L. Hoover Opera House, it hosts receptions and other gatherings.

Two horse-drawn carriages waited at the curb of the Santa Fe depot while a passenger train stood nearby. The south-central Kansas county was headed for its peak population of more than 12,000, which it reached in 1910.

Passenger trains no longer stop in Stafford — although one made an emergency stop in late 2011 when an ailing passenger needed hospital care.

Workers repaired a streetcar crossing at Minnesota Avenue and Fifth Street. Before automobile use became widespread, tens of thousands of people rode these cars around Kansas City, across the state line and out into the countryside. This view was north on Fifth. The car is marked "Quindaro Blvd"

Streetcar tracks and turn-of-the-century buildings have long been removed. A children's center stands on the right, and in the left background is the Robert J. Dole Federal Courthouse.

SENECA • about 1905

Like many other churches of various faiths, this Methodist congregation began its existence with a circuit-riding preacher. The group organized in 1858 and met in a member's home, in another church and in a school, sharing a minister with other Methodist congregations in northern Kansas and southern Nebraska. Seneca's Methodists built their own structure by the late 1870s, and in 1893 moved into this church at Seventh and Main streets. This and several other church spires mark the skyline of Seneca.

The Seneca United Methodist Church remains active in the 21st century. St. Mary's Catholic church, built about the same time, is imposing and well-attended; the former Unitarian church, which dates back to the late 1860s, was saved from demolition, restored and turned into the city library.

Beginning its life as a YMCA building in the heady development years of the late 1880s, this stone structure at First Street and Topeka was bought by the Masons in 1898, and remodeled.

As a Scottish Rite Temple, the stone building serves as a meeting place for the organization and for other groups.

The band played on, its stage a temporary stand built in in the middle of 11th and Boulevard streets. Advertisements dominated the scene; look at the band and you couldn't miss seeing a come-on for local merchants such as L.P.H. Hatch, a watchmaker who told potential customers that he was the local watch inspector for the Chicago, Rock Island & Pacific Railroad. The building behind the bandstand was constructed by John Keeran, a real estate agent.

Boulevard has been renamed Main Street and metal cladding and paint have altered the buildings. The Rock Island railroad no longer exists, and its route is now traveled by the Union Pacific.

Oregon Street was the main route through this Brown County town. The street was named for the Oregon Trail, which passed through this part of Kansas. Hiawatha was begun in territorial days, 1857, when the trail was still active. This view looks west.

Today Oregon Street is U.S. 36. The turreted building stands today, but with its arched entrance shifted west a few feet.

AUGUSTA
• 1907
and 2012

In the late 1800s, this south central Kansas community made its living largely through ranching and farming. The arrival of the railroad in the early 1880s helped in shipping products and boosting the town, but nothing contributed to its employment and general economy like the discovery of oil and natural gas fields in surrounding Butler County. For decades in the 20th century, refining operations provided an important number of jobs.

When refining operations ended in the 1980s, Augusta turned to other pursuits, among them a freshening up of its downtown.

A banker named Napoleon Bonaparte Brown bestowed this opera house on the city in 1907 and some accounts called it the most elegant between Kansas City and Denver. It staged musical plays, dances, recitals and high school graduations.

From the mid-1920s until 1974, it operated as a movie house. A marquee was added and side doors were covered to display movie bills.

As a 1976 U.S. Bicentennial project, the theater was bought, money raised and restoration begun, first of the exterior and then the interior. The Brown Grand Theatre staged a grand reopening in 1980, featuring the same play "The Vanderbilt Cup" that had opened the building in 1907. The theater is used by various community groups, from businesses and churches to community actors.

GREENSBURG • 1908

MAIN STREET, GREENSBURG, KAN

This southwest Kansas town was named for a stagecoach operator, Donald "Cannonball" Green, who is said to have had Carry Nation as a passenger. As the story goes, Nation once objected to Green's cigar, grabbed it from his mouth and threw it to the roadside. He stopped the carriage, lifted her off and left her to walk. This view looked north on Greensburg's Main Street from Florida Avenue.

Devastated by a tornado in 2007, Greensburg is rebuilding with modern structures designed to be energy-efficient — "green." The brick building at right, built in 1915, was the only one on the block, and one of few in town, to survive the twister. A block to the north is the main highway through town, U.S. 54.

Fred Harvey restaurants and hotels lined the Santa Fe tracks from Kansas City to California, and the Bisonte in Hutchinson was a grand one. Designed by Kansas City architect Louis Curtiss, one of several he did for the Fred Harvey company, this was named after the Bison that once flourished in Kansas. The presence of salt deposits and the city's salt industry made Hutchinson one of the larger stations along the Santa Fe.

The Bisonte closed in 1946 and was demolished in the 1960s to make way for a Holiday Inn. Although the chain did not build a motel here, Ramada Inn did.

Strong, Cy. Kas.

When the Santa Fe chose its route west of Emporia, it bypassed Cottonwood Falls and built a depot here, about a mile and a half north. A community grew up around the spot, first called Cottonwood Station and then in 1881 Strong City, after a Santa Fe official. Because Cottonwood Falls was the seat of Chase County, it remained important; the distance between the station and the county seat, however, was daunting for walkers. So an interurban streetcar line was established in 1886 by investors from both towns. Its cars were drawn by horses. In this scene, it passed the Bank Hotel on Cottonwood Avenue just north of the Santa Fe tracks.

The horsedrawn cars were replaced by a gasoline-engine car in the late 1910s, but the line began to lose money and was closed in 1920. The Bank Hotel has been demolished.

Drug Store and Post Office, Dorrance, Kans.

When he was 15 years old, L.W. Halbe began taking pictures with a small box camera, eventually recording 1,500 scenes in his hometown, Dorrance, and surrounding Russell County in central Kansas. This one shows a drugstore and post office, both near the railroad tracks. The two-horse postal delivery wagon was hitched up and the wheels were covered with mud, indicating that it had just returned from delivering mail.

The stone walls of the drugstore building survive although the rear portion has been removed, and the post office is long gone. The church building in the right background stands, but without its steeple.

It looks like a summer day in this town in south central Kansas; the women are wearing white blouses and dresses, the men are in their shirtsleeves and stores have deployed their awnings. The Peabody State Bank occupied a prominent site on the corner, as banks did in many towns. Mennonites helped populate this part of central Kansas in the 1870s, along with tenant farmers under a land system devised by William Tully, a large landowner.

Although the stone above the entrance reads, "Kansas State Bank," the business now operating in the corner building is Sharon's Korner Kitchen, a restaurant and caterer.

Coal fields and zinc deposits covered much of the land in southeast Kansas, southwest Missouri and northeast Oklahoma, and at the turn of the century miners were busy extracting the minerals. Pittsburg became a center of zinc smelting.

The mineral deposits have been worked out and the smelters have disappeared without much trace. The area has been reclaimed and now comprises a rental yard and other businesses on North Broadway just south of 29th Street.

Pittsburg has preserved a sizable amount of the streetscape north and south of its historic major intersection. This panorama begins at left, looking south on Broadway from Fourth Street and swings 180 degrees to look north on Broadway, at right. The Globe building, to the left, has disappeared, but many of the buildings on the west side of Broadway remain. To the right, for many blocks along Broadway, the scene today is surprisingly similar to that of 1909 — at least in the matter of structures.

In 2012, a foundation was restoring the theater marked by the Fox sign in hopes that it would spark more restoration in downtown Pittsburg. The movie house opened as the Colonial Theater in 1920, and so did not appear in its current form in the 1909 panorama.

1910-1919

The Butler County Courthouse was built in 1908 and 1909, and the fountain in the foreground, left, was added in memory of Thomas Benton Murdock, an El Dorado newspaper editor and politician. Among other things, the new courthouse included a farmer's rest area for farmers and their families, including a bathroom, and a separate room for the Grand Army of the Republic — Union veterans of the Civil War.

Above: A great field of oil was discovered in the mid-1910s and soon Butler County was dotted by oil derricks. The business of land records and leases filled the courthouse. Refineries large and small sprang up, too. The courthouse now boasts a new addition.

From the looks of things, the automobile owners of Sherman County have turned out for a parade. A photographer, trying to achieve a bird's-eye angle on the festivities, perched herself and her camera atop a cabinet, which rested atop a wagon. Her camera was pointed north on Franklin Avenue. In the 1910s, Thomas County was not two decades old, and boasted about 4,500 residents.

One building is the only visible remnant of a century's change, the four-window brick structure at left. The automobile, of course, is on constant parade. The county has long produced wheat and sorghum and, with irrigation, corn.

The First National Bank of Seneca opened in 1890, when the population of surrounding Nemaha County had rocketed to more than 19,000, a 50 percent increase over the 1880 count. Unlike similar bank buildings with a turret at the corner, the turret was not used as an entrance but as an office.

A coffee house now occupies the round corner of the old bank building in this view, which is to the east on Main Street from Fifth Street. Today, the county population is about 10,000, or half its peak in 1900.

The North Star Drug Store liberally advertised a tonic called Wa-Hoo, said to help with rheumatism, catarrh, kidney and stomach ailments: "Every bottle guaranteed." For the large number of Swedes in those parts, a sign above the door stated: "Svensk Apotek" or "Swedish Apothecary."

The upper floor of this building resembles its appearance of a century ago, but the ground-floor storefront, now an alterations and tailoring shop, has changed extensively. The store is on Santa Fe Avenue, Salina's main downtown street, just south of Iron Avenue.

Sunday afternoons in Brown County in the early 20th century — when the weather was pleasant — brought a concert at the city band shell in Horton. The musical fare typically consisted of marches and hymns.

Except for the disappearance of the band shell, little has changed behind the buildings on this block, the front sides of which face Eighth Street.

The builder of this modest hotel in southwest Kansas had built his own life on the plains from scratch. William P. Bunyan moved to Kansas from Illinois in the early 1880s, filed a claim in Meade County in 1884 and for the next few years lived in a dugout. He raised cattle, bought and sold land and by the turn of the century had accumulated a nice fortune. The Hotel Bunyan was only one of his many enterprises.

Its paint is peeling and some boards are missing, but the century-old frame building still stands. Meade County's population now is not much different from a century ago, when the Hotel Bunyan was operating.

Sugar beets boomed as a crop in the early 20th century, bringing massive processing plants like that of the United States Sugar and Land Company to this southwestern Kansas town. This plant, opened in 1906, brought new jobs, and also new immigrants, many from Mexico.

The factory closed in 1955, its machinery outdated. Sugar beets, dependent on irrigation, are still grown in southwestern Kansas, but they are shipped to other processors. Today, only part of the old plant remains.

Two men drove a herd of sheep south along a dusty road in rural Lenexa, Kansas. The tiny Johnson County town had livestock pens only a few hundred feet north of this spot, along the St. Louis & San Francisco Railroad tracks. Although

Lenexa was platted and settled in 1869, it was not incorporated until 1907, a few years before this photograph was made.

Pflumm Road is now a busy thoroughfare for Lenexa and cities north and south of it. Ninety-fifth Street crosses in the distance to the south. Some old farm homes remain along Pflumm, among them two-story house just left of center in the photograph on the facing page. It is barely visible behind large trees in this image.

Teenager L.W. Halbe of Dorrance ventured to the county seat one autumn day to capture images of Russell. From Seventh Street, he photographed this view of the east side of Main Street on a Wednesday afternoon. As in many Kansas towns in the days before busy automobile traffic, a gazebo stood in the middle of the street.

The city now boasts the economic boon of oil locally, along with its being the hometown of former U.S. Senator Bob Dole, the Republican candidate for president in 1996. The gazebo is gone from the intersection today, but several of the buildings on the east side remain. Note how the corner building has a newer façade than it had on the facing page, but the rest of the structure is the same.

OSAGE CITY • 1912 and 2012

A Santa Fe depot sat at the heart of this coal-mining hub, population about 2,400. The depot, which replaced a wooden depot, was in only its second year at the time of this photograph. By then Osage City was more than four decades old, platted after the Santa Fe had decided the route of its railroad. Although Osage City was the largest town in Osage County and bore the county name, the seat was in Lyndon, eight miles east.

The last regularly scheduled passenger train stopped here in 1968. The railroad eventually turned the depot over to the Osage County Historical Society, which later turned it over to the city. Restored with a grant from the Kansas Department of Transportation, the building is now a museum, and part is rented out for social occasions.

Men gathered at a row of car to give the vehicles a going-over in the 200 block of North Main Street. One man in driving cap and goggles is involved in a discussion with three other men, while a larger group forms around the right rear wheel of an uncovered car. This suggests that the cars were part of a promotion, a caravan or cross-country race meant to popularize automobiles and boost Newton as a highway hub.

Most of the buildings standing in 1910 remain today. The automobiles have changed considerably.

SCOTT CITY • 1911

Scott. City. Kans.

For Independence Day, a marching band trooped down the dirt Main Street of Scott City, followed by flag-flying motor cars and a large canopied wagon. Besides the country's independence, the Fourth of July in 1911 was the eve of the 25th anniversary of Scott County's organization. A rarity among western Kansas counties, there was never a battle over the seat, which was here.

Today, the major employers in Scott City are cattle feeders, and hay and cattle trucks are a common site on the highway through town. Today, Main Street carries U.S. 83.

When telephone use exploded after the turn of the century, companies met the demand by installing more and more phone lines — one per customer. This led to astounding scenes like this, in which the wires nearly blocked the view.

The mishmash of phone wires was solved by technological advances. Today, telephone lines are often buried underground and the growth of cell phone use means fewer land lines of any kind.

Surveyors studied the bank of the Kansas River at Kansas City for construction of a flood-prevention system for the low-lying Armourdale District. In the background, St. John's church rose above the Strawberry Hill neighborhood, where many Slavic immigrants and their descendants lived.

The Kansas River flood of 1951 overwhelmed the flood-prevention measures built in the early part of the century and Armourdale again suffered from high waters, requiring even more work in the years since. Strawberry Hill lives on as a historic area, although many homes were destroyed when Interstate 70 was built through the district in the 1950s.

Like its sister city in Missouri, Kansas City developed boulevards and parks and one feature was this sunken garden and fountain reached by steps from street level. The landscape architects created this as part of Waterway Park, staggered parcels running from Grandview Boulevard almost half a mile north to Washington Boulevard. This parcel lay between Minnesota and State avenues, Waterway Drive and 11th Street, just west of downtown

Evidently because the sunken garden had become a chore to maintain, the city filled it in the 1920s or 1930s. Today, only a small part of the original stone wall that formed the southeast corner of the garden remains visible at upper left.

GARNETT • about 1910 and 2012

The transition from horses to automobile was under way in Garnett. A two-horse carriage waited at the curb on the far side of the Anderson County Courthouse square. Automobiles were parked nearby and, on the far side of the street, an auto garage and service center announced its grand opening.

The bandstand has been rebuilt in masonry, but winter still holds down the number of people out for a stroll.

Students at the Kansas State Agricultural College lined up outside the Co-Op Bookstore a block from the entrance to campus. They were said to have been waiting to reserve tickets for a lecture.

A bookstore still operates in the location, which has become part of an eating and drinking district called Aggieville.

Henry Fromme, who farmed near Mullinville in southwest Kansas, was proud of his 28 draft horses and his registered Percheron stallion, so in 1912 he asked a local carpenter to build them a fine stable. This was the result — a 16-sided barn thought to be more wind resistant, more space-efficient and more economical with lumber than average barns. It was also more expensive. Henry posed outside it with his son Moritz. The barn was 70 feet in diameter and 50 feet tall at its peak. It contained a granary in the middle.

With the advent of tractors, draft horses became obsolete and so did the barn. Eventually, its owners stored hay in it and finally in 1993 donated it to the Kiowa County Historical Society. It was restored in 1995 with help from a Heritage Trust Fund grant. The Fromme-Birney Barn's centennial was marked in 2012.

The brand-new public library, built with a $75,000 gift from Andrew Carnegie, stood proudly on South Main Street. Behind it stood the tower of another local institution, the city jail.

The old library building has been nicely preserved, although as in many cities the surroundings have changed. In 1967 the library moved to a new building on the west side of Main. This building has since been used for municipal court sand for a science museum. In 2006, leaders of Fidelity Bank paid for a thorough restoration of the structure, and now use it as headquarters for the bank's commercial banking division.

There was little indication when this picture was made that Avenue A through Cimarron would become a major east-west highway within 20 years. It lay on a route between Garden City and Dodge City.

When U.S. highways were numbered to make travel easier for increasing numbers of motorists, Avenue A became part of U.S. 50 South. Today, it is named U.S. 50. The gable-front house at left has survived as a bed and breakfast.

Nazareth Academy, Concordia, Kans.

About two decades after arriving in Concordia, the Sisters of St. Joseph needed a new and larger convent, so they raised money and built this structure, the Nazareth Convent and Academy, in 1902 and 1903.

This brick and stone structure still is a home for the Sisters of St. Joseph, and serves as a residence for nuns who have retired.

Heavy June rains flooded the streets of this northeast Kansas town, sending enough water down the gutter to turn it into a temporary canal. This group floated up to a city water fountain for a whimsical photo: water, water, everywhere!

The city has built storm sewers and other diversions to carry water away from Main Street. The same intersection today no longer features the water fountain, or the gazebo in mid-street.

Like similar stations in other cities, Union Station created a single passenger terminal for various railroads serving Wichita. In May 1913, this station opened for business beside the elevated tracks over Douglas Avenue. It contained a Fred Harvey lunch and dining room until the middle 1930s.

Union Station no longer serves passenger trains; Amtrak stopped using the route in 1979 and today its nearest stop is in Newton. The building stands on the edge of what is now the Old Town entertainment district and near a new city arena.

John and Mary Veselik, immigrants from Bohemia in southeastern Europe, moved to this land in 1885. It lies southwest of Goodland and about nine miles east of the Colorado border. The Veseliks first lived in sod structures and then, in the late 1910s, built a farmhouse, outbuildings and this massive barn. The barn, a local landmark, was rented out for dances and other occasions. Music was provided sometimes by bands from as far as Denver and sometimes by a piano pushed up a ramp into the hayloft.

In 1952, a tornado severely damaged the barn and it was rebuilt, but only in part. A remnant of the old foundation, marking the western end of the barn before the tornado struck, still stands at left. Nothing else remains of the Veselik farmstead except the milk house and a plum thicket.

NEWTON

TRUCK ROOM

1920-1938

The Atchison, Topeka & Santa Fe began laying rails southwest from Topeka in autumn 1868 and by summer 1871 had reached Newton. From that point on, railroading proved a mainstay of the Newton economy, providing not only transportation but jobs in the shops established here. This station, the third built by the Santa Fe in Newton, and its attached Arcade Hotel were photographed in 1929, left. The Fred Harvey Company operated the food and newsstand services inside.

Above, in 2012, the station still serves passengers, now on Amtrak. The surrounding yards still perform maintenance on rail cars and locomotives – now operated by BNSF, for Burlington Northern Santa Fe — and the Sizemore, Burns & Gillmore law firm occupies the former Fred Harvey restaurant space.

Wallace County, which adjoins the Colorado border, was organized in 1868 but then in 1879 dissolved for lack of population. After a series of court decisions, opinions by the attorney general and elections, the county was finally reorganized in 1889. The towns of Wallace and Sharon Springs fought to become the county seat and in the end Sharon Springs won. In 1914 it built this courthouse.

Wallace County reached its peak population of 2,800 in 1930. The 2010 census found fewer than 1,500 residents.

American flags lined Santa Fe Avenue and people crowded the sidewalks on this busy afternoon in the early 20th century. The view is north from Iron Avenue.

Like most cities, Salina development has spread beyond the old city core, yet downtown is still active.

Faced in Kansas limestone and locally produced brick, the Brunswick Hotel was built in the late 1880s. It had 33 rooms. Guests could choose the American plan with meals included for $2 a day or the European plan for room only at 75 cents a day. The postcard was hand-tinted for reproduction in color.

After World War II, the structure was sold to the American Legion and then went through a variety of uses and owners — warehouse, private club, bed and breakfast, offices and private residence. The third floor, which had fallen into disrepair, was removed in 1976.

Many towns in Kansas boast wide main streets, but Plains says its is the widest — more than 155 feet from storefronts on one side to storefronts on the other. The surveyors who laid out Grand Avenue claimed, perhaps in jest, that the ground wouldn't be good for anything else. Before the late 1920s, when the street was paved, cars simply parked in the middle, along the row of utility poles.

This southwest Kansas community of more than 1,000 has built a brick median with trees and planters down Grand Avenue.

This new highway linked rural communities in Johnson County to the Rosedale District in Kansas City, and was expected to be an economic boon. Here, the brick pavement was being installed through downtown Lenexa. Grand opening ceremonies took place September 12 in Olathe, featuring a bricklaying contest won by "Indian Jim" Brown of the crew that built the 18-mile road.

The brick has long since been paved over. Today this road through Lenexa is called Santa Fe Trail Drive. It was rerouted through the old downtown in 1990 to make way for additional parking in front of businesses.

KU's Memorial Stadium is said to be the oldest on a college campus west of the Mississippi River. It opened in 1921, dedicated to university students who fought and died in the first World War. In 1925, the year this photograph was made, the stands had been extended to the south. The occasion was the homecoming football game. Two years later, the bowl at the north end was built, and in the 1960s the east and west stands were expanded. Succeeding decades brought a bigger pressbox and scoreboard and also new football offices, left.

Replete with student lounges and a ballroom, the Kansas Memorial Union was finished in 1927. Together with the football stadium, it was meant to honor students who died in World War I.

Through the years, the union has been expanded over and over, often in contrasting architectural style. In April 1970, in an era marked by vigorous student protests, the building burned.

The six sons of David and Ida Eisenhower posed on the front porch of the family home in Abilene, a smallish two-story frame house on the poorer side of the tracks. The brothers would accomplish much in their lives, none more than the brother sitting on the steps in Army uniform with shiny boots. Dwight D. Eisenhower would rise to five-star general and two-term president of the United States.

The Eisenhower home is preserved on the grounds of the Dwight D. Eisenhower Presidential Library and Museum. The house seemed small even to Dwight Eisenhower, who once joked that he had more space in his Pentagon office than there was in the house where he grew up.

LAWRENCE
• 1920s

By its sixth decade, the University of Kansas had assumed a collegiate appearance. Spooner Library, left, was finished in 1894. One year later Blake Hall, in the distance beyond Spooner, opened and in 1902 Dyche Museum, right, was completed. Fraser Hall, in the background at right, dated to the early 1870s. Although the designs of the buildings differed, they shared red roofs and limestone walls.

LAWRENCE
• 2012

Jayhawk Boulevard has been widened for increased traffic, and old Blake and old Fraser have been demolished. Their replacements, bearing the same names, were built in the 1960s.

This stucco depot of the Chicago, Rock Island & Pacific railroad replaced a wooden one destroyed by fire in 1910. Seward County, of which Liberal is the seat, had fewer than 10,000 residents when this picture was taken.

The Chamber of Commerce and the city's Economic Development agency use the old depot, which was restored in 1998, for offices. A Veterans Administration clinic occupies the restored Grier Eating House and Cimarron Hotel. Seward County's population, most of which lives in Liberal, has grown to almost 23,000. Wheat and other crops, oil and gas and trucking are major industries.

Haskell Indian Institute dedicated its new football stadium with its notable World War I memorial entrance arch in October 1926. Construction money was donated by Native Americans and the dedication weekend drew representatives from tribes across the country. The school was established by the federal government in 1884 as a boarding school for students of various tribes, its aim to help Indians assimilate into majority American culture.

Now named Haskell Indian Nations University, the school has a thousand students and fields a men's football team along with men's and women's teams in basketball, soccer and other sports.

The Union Pacific reached this northeast Kansas town in 1867. A little more than 60 years later, the railroad opened a fancy new depot, and that was call for a celebration. A group of boys sat down at trackside with their opening-day ice cream and mugged for the photographer.

The lads in the 1928 photograph now would be well into their 80s, and that's also the age of this building, now vacant. The tracks have been removed and the railroad's main line has gone to a new rail yard and train-crew terminal on the northwest edge of town. The Union Pacific remains a major area employer.

A display of new washing machines stood in the 900 block of Broadway, the prime business street of this northeast Kansas town. Fred Haar, owner of the store, stood at right and his salesman at left. The storefront signs boasted that traincar loads of washers had been sold in Marysville, so no better proof was needed of the machines' quality. Another sign listed the radio stations on which Maytag-sponsored programs could be heard.

Where Haar Electric once sold washing machines, a health service operates today.

In the countryside between the unincorporated community of Overland Park and the village of Stanley ran this stretch of U.S. 69, the major highway to Fort Scott. In the distance to the north, the graded road dipped to cross branches of Tomahawk Creek.

U.S. 69 and Metcalf Avenue have been moved west, and this stretch of street just north of 135th is called Old Metcalf Avenue. Office buildings and shopping centers have popped up all around, but a 19th-century cemetery still tops the hill behind the retaining wall at right.

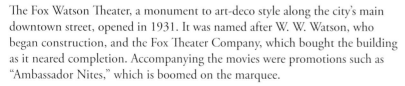

The Fox Watson Theater, a monument to art-deco style along the city's main downtown street, opened in 1931. It was named after W. W. Watson, who began construction, and the Fox Theater Company, which bought the building as it neared completion. Accompanying the movies were promotions such as "Ambassador Nites," which is boomed on the marquee.

In the late 1980s the movie house closed and its owner, Dickinson Theatres, donated it to the city. After a restoration, it reopened as a concert hall called the Stiefel Theatre in 2003.

The Besse Hotel, just off the city's prime downtown intersection, was opened in 1927.

The Besse closed in 1970 and reopened three decades later in 2010 with low- and moderate-income apartments.

The Old Dutch Mill was one of a group of attention-getting gasoline stations built along major highways in Kansas beginning in the late 1920s. Often these stations had tourist cabins, too. Besides this one on U.S. 40 in Salina, windmill stations operated in Marysville, Seneca, Lindsborg, Kansas City, and at Victory Junction on the boundary between Wyandotte and Leavenworth counties. On this day, the Salina station was making a show of it; waitresses were decked out in Dutch maid costumes, cars lined up at the pumps, mechanics lined up to serve them and a car sat on the outdoor lift.

Often, one gasoline station replaces another and that's what happened at Santa Fe and Pacific avenues in the north part of Salina. The windmill structure was torn down in the 1960s and replaced by a one-story station. Although gasoline pumps are gone, the site continues in the auto business.

The city's most famous resident, journalist and author William Allen White, stood with his wife, Sallie Lindsay White, in front of their home at 927 Exchange Street. Political and literary celebrities visited the Whites here, among them Theodore Roosevelt, Edna Ferber and Frank Lloyd Wright. The Whites had lived since 1899 in the house, which featured walls of sandstone and red brick and was nicknamed "Red Rocks."

Now named the William Allen White State Historic Site, the house can be toured by the public. A visitor center is on the grounds.

A golfer teed up the ball at the Municipal Golf Course, which used the ground of the old Fort Hays military reservation. The stone blockhouse, rear, dating to the late 1860s, was meant as a defensive retreat, but the fort was never attacked. At the time of this photograph, it was the clubhouse for golfers.

A golf course still adjoins the grounds of the Fort Hays State Historic Site, but the blockhouse is no longer part of the recreation area. The officers' quarters behind the blockhouse originally stood where they are today, but had been sold and moved off the property when the 1930 photograph was made.

Sitting amidst a vast wheat-growing area, Hays for years not only shipped grain but also milled it. The Hays City Flour mill, which was established in the early 1870s and began using the Hays City name in 1910, advertised its Semolino brand, "From Kansas Choice Turkey Red Wheat." That was the variety introduced in the 1870s by German settlers from Russia. The grain had advantages over the soft wheat previously grown, among them better resistance to cold, insects and disease.

The mill stood into the 1980s but has since been demolished.

When the Methodists of this south-central Kansas town decided to build a new church, they sought out an architect from Wichita, Don Buel Schuler. He gave them something far different from the Gothic Revival building it replaced. On the outside, he created a streamlined, Collegiate Gothic look. Inside, the sanctuary drew inspiration from Frank Lloyd Wright's Unity Temple in Oak Park, Illinois. Schuler, who had designed a Wichita church that impressed the building committee, had once worked for Wright. The church was dedicated in 1927.

The congregation is smaller than when the church was built, but has maintained the building and holds regulars services there.

Automobiles jammed Main Street of this central Kansas town, where business from the surrounding oil fields and royalties paid to farmers helped stave off the worst effects of the Great Depression.

The city continues to do well economically and lists more than 55 industries with offices there. McPherson County has grown slowly but steadily and now counts more than 29,000 residents.

The Lamer Hotel, three years old, rose over the east side of Main Street in this view, which was to the north from 11th Street. The Lamer was part of a group that also operated hotels in Salina and Abilene. Predating the Lamer were the Mulroy Hotel, built in 1889, and the Strand movie theater and Basgall grocery store, both built in 1917.

Three of the four buildings remain; only the oldest, the Mulroy Hotel, has been demolished.

This stone shelter atop Coronado Heights in central Kansas was built by employees of the federal Work Projects Administration. A road winds up to it and stone picnic areas sit at the crest of the hill. The Spanish explorer Francisco Vasquez de Coronado explored parts of what is now Kansas in the 1500s, and local boosters named the hill after him. Until the 1920s, this and other hills nearby were simply called "Smoky Hill Buttes."

Visitors still come to Coronado Heights for recreation and a sweeping view of central Kansas. Lindsborg in McPherson County lies just to the south.

Southwest Kansas was part of the 1930s Dust Bowl, when drought, high temperatures and high winds scorched the land and created great clouds of dust. This blow struck Elkhart, in Morton County near the Oklahoma border, on May 21.

The 1930s depression cut the population of Morton County in half, to barely more than 2,000 people. Today, however, it numbers more than 3,000.

When this photograph was made, the Wichita Municipal Airport was on its way to becoming one of the country's busiest. Opened in 1935, it replaced a nearby hangar that served as the city's first airport. Right: This imprint, or cache, on an airmail envelope, marked the first airmail service from Wichita by way of Hutchinson and Garden City to Pueblo, Colorado in 1939.

For decades, aviation has been big business in Wichita. The private aircraft industry has been a major employer. In 1951, barely six months after the beginning of the Korean war, the Air Force established McConnell Air Force Base here and asked non-military traffic to stop using the building as soon as possible.

By 1954, all commercial flights had moved to a new airport that is now called Mid-Continent. This building was used until the 1980s by the Air Force. It is now home to the Kansas Aviation Museum and its extensive collection of vintage aircraft and memorabilia.

In the center of a row of businesses across from the Woodson County Courthouse square, the Temple theater was showing "Algiers" starring Charles Boyer. Also, it was advertising a national movie-quiz contest with a $50,000 first prize. In the 1930s, when Yates Center's economy centered on shipping hay and otherwise serving surrounding farms in southeast Kansas, the county population was about 8,500.

Woodson County in the most recent census had 3,309 residents, continuing a decline that began in the early 20th century. A preservation group is at work to keep up historic structures. The Temple theater no longer shows movies, having most recently been occupied by a religious group.

1940-

Between classes, students and faculty strolled past Anderson Hall, the administration building of what, in 1940, was called the Kansas State College of Agriculture and Applied Science. The north wing of Anderson Hall, closest in this view, left, was built in 1878 and 1879, the central portion with the tower in 1882 and the south wing in 1884.

The K-State campus is much larger today, but Anderson Hall, above right, continues as the most recognizable landmark on the campus of what is now Kansas State University. The institution has more than 22,000 students.

The Rorabaugh Buck Dry Goods Company stood at the left and S. H. Kress dime store at right at one of Wichita's busiest intersections. The view is to the south on Broadway across Douglas Avenue.

Rorabaugh Buck changed its name to Buck's in 1943 and closed in 1967. The building it occupied is gone, but the structures on the other three corners still stand where they did 70 years ago.

Sheridan Coliseum, built of local limestone, opened in 1917. This photograph probably was made in the 1940s. The building contained the gymnasium and auditorium of the western branch of the Kansas State Teacher's College. Today, it has been remodeled and renamed Sheridan Hall. The school is now Fort Hays State University.

Even as upper-middle-class houses were being completed in Westwood, in the distance in this view to the northwest, a combination produce and diary market, root beer stand and gasoline station was operating on U.S. 50 at Belinder Road.

The Fairway Shops, built in 1940 by the J. C. Nichols Company, stand at the corner of Belinder and busy Shawnee Mission Parkway. Fairway was incorporated in 1949.

This hotel opened in 1888 with 100 rooms and the name Inter-State. The builder, Charles W. Goodlander, had moved to Fort Scott in territorial days and made a fortune in contracting, banking and milling. In 1895, after the Inter-State proved a losing proposition to Goodlander and other investors, he bought the mortgage, renamed it after himself and operated it. It stood at the southwest corner of National Avenue and Wall Street.

In the 1950s, an oil company floated the idea of building a gasoline station on this corner. A group of business and professional people organized to save the site — not to preserve the Goodlander but to build a modern hotel. The group prevailed, demolished the Goodlander and in 1957 the Downtowner Motel opened at the spot, which was then the intersection of U.S. 54 and 69.

Grat Hollenberg set up shop along the Oregon Trail in 1854 just as Kansas became a territory. His aim was to sell goods to travelers setting out from Independence and Westport, Missouri. In 1857, as trail traffic leaving St. Joseph, Missouri, grew, he moved to this spot near Hanover in north central Kansas.

During the brief life of the Pony Express, Hollenberg also served its riders and horses. After that venture and as trail traffic diminished, Hollenberg turned his attention to farming. He died in 1874 and the residence was turned over to the state in 1941. This photograph was made two years later, after restoration.

Now more than a century and a half old, this structure and the land around it are preserved and operated by the Kansas Historical Society as the Hollenberg Pony Express Station, a state historic site.

In an era of lingering segregation in Kansas, the two-room Walker Elementary handled 44 black children. The school, which stood in the unincorporated South Park community in northern Johnson County, had no indoor plumbing and was equipped with hand-me-down equipment from other schools. A new school, South Park Elementary, was being built nearby, one with indoor plumbing, separate teachers and classrooms for each grade and an auditorium. But in those days, when larger Kansas districts were allowed to maintain "separate but equal" schools, the tiny South Park restricted the new building to white children only. Encourage by while allies and helped by the NAACP, Walker parents sued. In 1949 the Kansas Supreme Court ruled that black children must be allowed to attend the new school.

South Park now is part of Merriam, and the former school building on West 50th Terrace has been modified over time. It now houses the Philadelphia Missionary Baptist Church. A plaque nearby commemorate the late 1940s desegregation effort in the area.

These chalk towers in western Kansas, known as Monument Rocks, formed the floor of a sea that once covered this part of the world. They are a type of limestone, the particles of which precipitated from the sea water. When the sea disappeared, erosion began, forming these striking shapes. Geologists have named this the Niobrara Formation, and it contained numerous fossils of mosasaurs and other swimming reptiles of the Cretaceous Period — which ended 65 million years ago.

This Kansas landmark, which is on private land, can be visited by the public. Fossils are harder to find in the 21st century, however, because the land has been picked over.

The Fairmont Ice Cream Store on the corner of South Jefferson Avenue and East Street advertised a double-dip cone for a nickel.

The old ice cream store is occupied by a child and youth services agency. The population of the town surrounding it is about 5,700 today.

The 600 block of Minnesota Avenue was bustling this spring day. All storefronts were occupied, most with retailers. The population of Kansas City had grown to 165,000, an increase of 14 percent since 1940 and things looked bright for future growth.

Few retailers are open today along Minnesota Avenue. Some blame the Center City Mall, an urban renewal project of the early 1970s, which remade the street into a series of winding, one-lane paths for vehicles and concrete protrusions for pedestrians. At Seventh Street, to the left in this photograph, which looks west, stainless steel pylons were erected. Each was five feet square and 20 feet tall. After seven years of heavy criticism, the pylons were removed. In the early 1980s, the mall was ripped out and Minnesota returned to a semblance of its old self. The 2010 census put the city's population at about 145,000.

After World War II, the popularity of Kansas State basketball created a need for a bigger gym than Nichols Hall, and in 1951 Ahearn Field House was under construction adjacent to the football stadium, which was called Memorial Stadium. When it was finished, Ahearn seated 11,700. It was named for Michael F. Ahearn, a former athletics director and coach.

No longer is Ahearn or the football stadium used for major intercollegiate basketball or football. Basketball games moved to the new Bramlage Coliseum in 1988 and volleyball and indoor track are played in Ahearn. Football moved to a new stadium in 1967. The old football stadium is used now for club soccer, rugby and marching band practice. The interior of the stands has been made into offices.

East First Avenue was a busy place this day with cars parked to the right, to the left and down the middle. In the middle of the block to the left stood the Fox, a 1,200-seat art-deco movie palace going on 20 years old. It was showing "About Face" starring Gordon McRae and Eddie Bracken. Farther east, across Walnut Street, stood the Soldiers and Sailors Monument, dedicated in 1919 to Union veterans of the Civil War and topped by a figure of Abraham Lincoln.

Much has changed in 60 years, but not the Fox or the Soldiers and Sailors monument. In 1955, the Fox showed the world premiere of "Picnic," starring William Holden and Kim Novak. The movie was set in Kansas and based on the play by Kansan William Inge. The Fox closed in 1985, but was restored by a non-profit group and reopened in 1999.

The Jefferson County Courthouse, built only two years after the Civil War ended, had recently celebrated its centennial and was the longest continuously operating courthouse in Kansas.

The old courthouse lasted only two years after the 1958 photograph was made. A tornado ripped through Oskaloosa, damaging the building. Its replacement, a modest brick one-story courthouse, opened in 1962.

CONCORDIA • 1960

The Union Pacific railroad reached this north-central Kansas town in early 1878. The next year it built a frame depot that was replaced by this one about 1917. The new depot was simple and based on a standard plan used by the railroad. Like most stations of that era, separate waiting rooms were created, one for men and one for women and children. Two other railroads served Concordia and also built depots, the Missouri Pacific and the Santa Fe. The Chicago, Burlington & Quincy maintained a freight office.

Tracks used by the Union Pacific at the depot were removed in the late 1960s and early 1970s, and the station was donated for use as a museum. It has been reopened to show the history of the orphan train movement, in which charity institutions placed orphaned, abandoned and homeless children from the East Coast in new homes throughout the country. The children traveled on the railroad and their journeys were eventually called "orphan trains." The era began in the second half of the 19th century and ended about 1929. An estimated 200,000 children found new homes as a result of it.

One of the –
World's Largest

In most Kansas towns, the grain elevator is the tallest structure; in Hutchinson, the length is the thing. Half a mile long, this at times has been called the world's largest grain elevator and at other times one of the largest. Either way, its size is astonishing. Construction began in 1952 and grain was first stored in it in 1953 — yet it was only half as big as this. The elevator prospered, so its owners doubled the size by 1961.

The elevator has changed owners, but it still operates. Employees have used bicycles to move through the room atop the grain bins.

CIMARRON • early 1960s

This hotel on North Main Street opened in 1886, the year before Gray County was organized. Even then, a "county seat war" was fought between Ingalls and Cimarron, ending in a victory for the latter in 1889 — and probably creating additional future customers for this hotel. The building, designed in the French Second Empire style, was meant as an investment for a Dodge City judge. In the beginning it was named the New West. Briefly in the 1890s it was used as a health resort with cures for various ills, but returned to lodging in the early 1900s.

The Cimarron Hotel remains in operation with guest rooms, just off the highway that leads west to Garden City and east to Dodge City in southwest Kansas. Gray County's population peaked in 1939 at just under 7,000 and since has dropped to about 2,700.

Beckoned by land promoters, 300 black people left Kentucky in 1877 to begin new lives in Kansas. Joined by a score or more of blacks from eastern Kansas, their journey ended here, in Graham County in northwest Kansas. The immigrants spent their first winter in dugouts but soon began building a town. Stores, churches, a hotel and a school sprang up. Hopes were dimmed in the late 1880s, however, when the railroad bypassed Nicodemus; some residents moved away. More left in the Great Depression of the 1930s. Among the first group of immigrants to Nicodemus, one year old at the time, was Jerry Scruggs. At 88 years old, he showed what was left of the colony to a reporter and photographer for *The Kansas City Times.* The vacant Masonic hall stood at right, and a former grocery at left.

Made a National Historic Site in the 1990s, Nicodemus has a museum and visitors center in the old township hall, out of sight to the right in this photograph. The Masonic Hall and grocery are gone, but five historic structures still stand — two churches, a school building and a hotel, all built from 1881 to 1907, and the township hall, built in 1939. Nicodemus is the oldest surviving black pioneer town west of the Mississippi. Once a year on the last weekend of July, it celebrates a homecoming for current and former residents and their families.

Before the completion of Interstate 35, this road was U.S. 50, the major highway between Kansas City and south-central Kansas. Farms like this one southwest of Ottawa saw cars and trucks a-plenty, day and night.

The official designation of U.S. 50 has moved. Traffic speeds by on I-35 a mile or so to the north, and this has become a country road.

Throughout the history of Kansas, tornadoes have been a fact of life. Many towns have suffered and some have been nearly wiped out by twisters, but none had hit the capital city until this one the evening of June 8, 1966. It ripped through the heart of the city, destroying homes and buildings, badly damaging the campus of Washburn University and just missing the state Capitol —although it caused some damage to the dome. In the aftermath, a photographer captured the scene on Kansas Avenue north from 11th Street. In all, 16 people died and more than 500 were injured. It was one of the costliest tornadoes in American history.

Older buildings damaged by the tornado were torn down and some replaced by state buildings such as the Curtis State Office Building and its parking garage at left. The 1966 tornado put an end to a local legend that Burnett's mound, a rise in southwest Topeka, would protect the city from tornadoes. In fact, the tornado passed right over the mound.

In an attempt to improve their downtowns and energize their economies, several Kansas cities in the late 1960s and early 1970s laid plans to re-route streets, create malls, add sidewalk canopies and otherwise modernize aging business districts. In November 1971, Parsons dedicated its urban renewal project, built with help from federal funds. George Romney, U.S. secretary of Housing and Urban Development, spoke at the gazebo built at the intersection of Main and 18th streets.

In most Kansas downtowns, the urban renewal projects had mixed success and in some they backfired, driving businesses and people away from downtowns. By the final decades of the 20th century, city after city was removing malls and other features. Today, this southeast Kansas town has mostly restored the scene on Main, looking east from 18th.

As they laid track across the arid west, the Santa Fe and Rock Island railroads needed water for the boilers of their steam locomotives. Greensburg obliged, building a new water system in the late 1880s that drew water from this well. Crews of 12 to 15 local people, in addition to people passing through and looking for work, went to work using shovels and picks. Stone was imported from 12 miles south for the well casing. The well reached 109 feet deep, to a layer of water-bearing gravel. In the 1930s, when its use for the city water system ended, the well was made a tourist attraction.

The tornado that wiped out most of the city in 2007 destroyed the tourist museum at the well. This new, circular structure was designed for it. For years, a large pallasite — a rare form of meteorite — was displayed at the museum. After the tornado, it was placed in the Greensburg City Hall.

In an era when old buildings often were viewed as beyond repair, demolition of this mill, built in 1879, was under way. In its final incarnation as a mill the structure was owned by the Newton Milling & Elevator Company. Before that it was owned by Bernhard Warkentin, a Russian immigrant who, in the 1800s, encouraged planting of "Turkey Red" hard winter wheat in Kansas. Warkentin's mill ground the new variety, which had higher yields and better resistance to the cold than previous strains in Kansas.

A local manufacturer and inventor bought the structure in 1973, halted its demolition and then oversaw its restoration. Today the building, which stands at Third and Main Streets, is called the Old Mill. It houses several businesses and a restaurant. Fire damaged it in 2009, but it has been put back into business.

Like many buildings in the city's historic downtown area, this structure at the northeast corner of Poyntz Avenue and Fourth Street has undergone wave after wave of remodeling to fit new tenants. Built in 1890 as the Eames Building, it housed the First National Bank and Keller's department store in the 1970s when the owners chose to modernize the look by adding an aluminum cover. The same happened in towns across the Midwest as landlords and merchants associations attempted to stay up to date with shopping centers and strip malls.

Aluminum skin was removed from the bank part of the building, in the 1980s. The rest came down in the 1990s. Keller's closed in 1983.

They don't make them like this anymore. Because stone was plentiful, Kansas bridge builders often turned to the material from the beginning of settlement to the 1930s. This bridge was built in 1936 by the Works Progress Administration, a New Deal Agency, and was one of the last of its kind.

It spans Bear Creek in the countryside six miles west and four miles north of tiny Richfield in Kansas' farthest southwestern county. Because the aim of the WPA was to create jobs and try to overcome the Great Depression, construction of the bridge was labor-intensive.

Now on the National Register of Historic Places, the bridge still carries a paved rural road over Bear Creek. Metal tubes mounted in concrete have been used to bolster the bridge, altering somewhat the appearance of the structure.

ACKNOWLEDGMENTS

All across Kansas — from state and university archives to public libraries to historical societies to individuals — we dealt with people who were helpful, friendly and genuinely interested in this project. Here are most of them, and if anyone was slighted by not being included, we sincerely apologize.

At the Kansas Historical Society, Lin Fredericksen, Nancy Sherbert, Barry Worley and the rest of the staff helped us accumulate scores of published images. The society's Kansas Memory website is an excellent help for doing research statewide.

Thanks also to Mary Nelson at Wichita State University Libraries, Kathy A. Lafferty at Spencer Research Library at the University of Kansas, Jamin Landavazo at the Reno County Museum, Linda Glasgow of the Riley County Historical Society, Jami Frazier Tracy of the Wichita-Sedgwick County Historical Museum, and many more, who are:

Mark Dulek, Crawford County Historical Museum; Roger Fitch, Omaha, Nebraska; Mary Ann Thompson, Hays Public Library; Mary Kay Menard, Leavenworth Public Library; Roger Shipman, Joe Hursey and Phil Reaka, Miami County Historical Museum; Laurie Oshel, Finney County Historical Society; Mary Adair, Biodiversity Institute, University of Kansas; Deborah Barker and Suzanne Geiss, Franklin County Records & Research Center, Ottawa; Lowell Beecher, Graham County Historical Society; Steve Read, McPherson Public Library; Marion and Wanda Hearn and Jean Fancher, Stafford County Historical Society; Laura McClung, Goodland Public Library; Chris Griffin and Ann Miner, Thomas County Historical Society; Debra Hiebert, Harvey County Historical Society; Lon Smith and Craig Parsons, Kansas Aviation Museum, Wichita; Ken Stallbaumer, Seneca, Kansas; Nancy Ohnick, Meade County Historical Museum; Bill Felber and Ned Seaton, *Manhattan Mercury*; David Boutros, The State Historical Society of Missouri Research Center-Kansas City; Bob Neier of Wichita, Tamina Fromme of Mullinville, Jim Crawley and the Kiowa County Historical Society; Richard Gannon, Topeka, Kansas; Bill Black, Dan Grigg Images, Omaha, Nebraska; Todd Crow, Lenexa Historical Society; Kathy Struss, Dwight D. Eisenhower Museum & Library; the staff of the Salina Public Library; the staff of the Watkins Community Museum of History in Lawrence; Chris Taylor, Atchison County Historical Society; Bill Fisher, Fort Scott National Historic Site; Robert Smith, Fort Riley Museum, and Pete Bussen and Thelma Jennings, Fort Wallace Museum.

As always, Derek Donovan and the staff of *The Kansas City Star* library pitched in with help and tolerance.

Finally, thanks to the friendly folks at Great Southern Bank in Paola: Cathy Flake, who got permission us to take pictures from the roof, and Doug Kiser, who helped us get up there.

ILLUSTRATION CREDITS

ILLUSTRATION CREDITS

County Historical Society
98. Kansas State Historical Society
100. David Nigh Collection, McPherson Public Library
102. Special Collections and University Archives, Wichita State University Libraries
104. Kansas State Historical Society
106. Files of *The Kansas City Star*
108. Stafford County Historical Society
110. The State Historical Society of Missouri Research Center-Kansas City
112. Kansas State Historical Society
114. Local History Section, Wichita Public Library
116. Goodland Public Library
118. Special Collections and University Archives, Wichita State University Libraries
119. Special Collections and University Archives, Wichita State University Libraries
120. Kansas State Historical Society
122. Special Collections and University Archives, Wichita State University Libraries
124. Courtesy of the Reno County Museum, Hutchinson, Kansas
126. Special Collections and University Archives, Wichita State University Libraries
128. Kansas State Historical Society
130. Special Collections and University Archives, Wichita State University Libraries
132. Kansas State Historical Society
134. Library of Congress Prints and Photographs Division Washington, D.C.
136. Files of *The Kansas City Star*
138. Thomas County Historical

Society
140. Ken Stallbaumer, Seneca, Kansas
141. Kansas State Historical Society
142. Kansas Collection, Spencer Research Library, University of Kansas Libraries
144. Special Collections and University Archives, Wichita State University Libraries
146. Finney County Historical Society
148. Lenexa Historical Society
150. Kansas State Historical Society
151. Special Collections and University Archives, Wichita State University Libraries
152. Harvey County Historical Society
154. Kansas State Historical Society
156. Kansas State Historical Society
158. Kansas State Historical Society
160. Kansas City, Kansas, Plans and Zoning
161. Kansas State Historical Society
162. Courtesy of the Riley County Historical Society
164. Bob Neier and the Kiowa County Historical Society
166. Local History Section, Wichita Public Library
168. Kansas State Historical Society
170. Authors' collection
172. Special Collections and University Archives, Wichita State University Libraries
174. Local History Section, Wichita Public Library
176. Kansas State Historical Society
178. Kansas State Historical Society
180. Kansas State Historical Society
182. Salina Public Library photo collection
184. Linn Peterson Collection, McPherson Public Library

186. Meade County Historical Museum
188. Lenexa Historical Society
190, top. University Archives, Spencer Research Library, University of Kansas Libraries
191, top. University Archives, Spencer Research Library, University of Kansas Libraries
192. Dwight D. Eisenhower Presidential Library and Museum
194. University Archives, Spencer Research Library, University of Kansas Libraries
196. Special Collections and University Archives, Wichita State University Libraries
198. Kansas State Historical Society
200. Kansas State Historical Society
202. Kansas State Historical Society
204. Courtesy Johnson County Museum
206. Kansas State Historical Society
207. Authors' collection
208. Salina Public Library photo collection
210. Emporia State University
212. Hays Public Library
214. Hays Public Library
216. Stafford County Historical Museum
218. Kansas State Historical Society
220. Hays Public Library
222. Kansas State Historical Society
224. Library of Congress Prints and Photographs Division, Washington, DC
226. Courtesy of the Kansas Aviation Museum, Wichita
228. Library of Congress Prints and Photographs Division Washington, DC
230-231. Courtesy of the Morse

Department of Special Collections, Kansas State University Libraries
232. Kansas State Historical Society
233. Hays Public Library
234. The State Historical Society of Missouri Research Center-Kansas City, J.C. Nichols scrapbooks)
236. Files of *The Kansas City Star*
238. Kansas State Historical Society
240. Johnson County Museum, Bill Curtis, photographer
242. Files of *The Kansas City Star*
244. Kansas State Historical Society
246. Files of *The Kansas City Star*
248. Files of *The Kansas City Star*
250. Courtesy of the Reno County Museum, Hutchinson, Kansas
252. Library of Congress Prints and Photographs Division Washington, DC
254. Kansas State Historical Society
256. Courtesy of the Reno County Museum, Hutchinson, Kansas, and Dan Grigg Images
258. Kansas State Historical Society
260. Files of *The Kansas City Star*
262. Kansas State Historical Society
264. Files of *The Kansas City Star*
266. Files of *The Kansas City Star*
268. Authors' collection
270. Harvey County Historical Society
272. *Manhattan Mercury* and Riley County Historical Society
274. National Register of Historic Places, National Park Service, U.S. Department of the Interior

INDEX

INDEX

INDEX

ABOUT THE AUTHOR AND PHOTOGRAPHERS

Jean and Monroe Dodd at Monument Rocks, Gove County, 2011. Photograph by Ed Dodd.

Monroe Dodd was an editor at *The Kansas City Times* and the *Kansas City Star* from 1976 to 2008. In 1999, he served as editor and project manager of *Kansas City: An American Story*, a history of Kansas City published by Kansas City Star Books. Since then, he has written *A Splendid Ride: The Streetcars of Kansas City 1871-1957* and *Christmastime in Kansas City: The Story of the Season*. He has also produced three volumes of *Kansas City Then & Now*, which compare long-ago Kansas City area scenes with the same scenes today. He graduated from the University of Kansas in 1971 with a bachelor of science in journalism and received a master of arts in history from KU in 1974. He lives in Shawnee, Kansas, with his wife, Jean Donaldson Dodd.

Jean Dodd was for more than 10 years the assistant managing editor for graphics and photography at the *Kansas City Star*. She then returned to the University of Kansas and received a bachelor of science in architectural studies and a master of architecture. She currently works as a design and construction project manager for the U.S. General Services Administration. Jean has designed all of the aforementioned Kansas City Star Books. She assisted Monroe in the making of this book and shot many of the photographs.